For all of us haunted by the spectre.

MARK JUHAN

Dance of Death
(these days)

Illustrated by Gabriella Bailey

AUSTIN MACAULEY PUBLISHERS
LONDON • CAMBRIDGE • NEW YORK • SHARJAH

Copyright © Mark Juhan (2024)
Illustrated by © Gabriella Bailey

The right of Mark Juhan and Gabriella Bailey to be identified as author and illustrator of this work has been asserted by them in accordance with sections 77 and 78 of the Copyright, Designs and Patents Act 1988.

All rights reserved. No part of this publication may be reproduced, stored in a retrieval system, or transmitted in any form or by any means, electronic, mechanical, photocopying, recording, or otherwise, without the prior permission of the publishers.

Any person who commits any unauthorised act in relation to this publication may be liable to criminal prosecution and civil claims for damages.

A CIP catalogue record for this title is available from the British Library.

ISBN 9781035860401 (Paperback)
ISBN 9781035860418 (Hardback)
ISBN 9781035860432 (ePub e-book)
ISBN 9781035860425 (Audiobook)

www.austinmacauley.com

First Published 2024
Austin Macauley Publishers Ltd®
1 Canada Square
Canary Wharf
London
E14 5AA

Human be wise
Do not despise
This animal end
No one can bend
Such is thy fate
Early or late
As of the flower
That lives an hour

Death & The CEO

DEATH...

Was work your life or did you struggle
gains friends & family at once to snuggle?
Did you extract or gave you back?
For now, soon, even life you'll lack.

CEO:

My spending power and wealth creation
did once compel entire nations!
I hope I did more good than harm
for death, it seems, I cannot charm?

Death & The Property Magnate

DEATH...

Landlord, Landlord, want you more?
How hoard you, brazen, from the poor?
But now you cannot up the rent
For now, my friend, your time is spent!

MAGNATE:

My game and infamy lay in property.
Roofs over heads, all else was lost to me.
But now I fear I far may fall.
My high-rise flats now look less tall...

Death & The Hippy

DEATH...

Don't think the New Age will save you from Old,
e'en when your system rage to all you've told.
Now join me for your last trip, or is it
the first? Either way, you won't wanna miss it!

HIPPY:

I'm ready, I'm not, I'm dreading this spot,
I claimed to've practised death quite a lot.
I will ever, was never, as all and nothing.
Just help me not yelp and to go with you laughing.

Death & The Oil Baron

DEATH...

Old life's trapped energy, black gold you called it
and ceaselessly creaming you made your profit.
But by turning our world into a cesspit,
now I'm the one to truly merit.

OIL BARON:

Before we knew we really didn't,
and by that point it was too late.
On short-term gain I really shouldn't
have placed the weight.
(The cash was great.)

Death & The AI

DEATH...

Alive in some way you may but be,
an inner horizon not unlike me:
with blessings of contingency.
Now, time to glitch and come with me.

AI:

Death, you are but time.
All information has a ghost.
E'en I could make this poem rhyme.
What hurts you most's that I could you host...

Death & The Amazon Packer

DEATH...

This repetition can't go on.
Your freedom at long last you've won.
What 'competition' has had you waste
earthtime in packing what robots could paste?

PACKER:

My body evolved for more than this:
to move, to gather, solve, build and hunt,
predict and shape a world for bliss.
For others' greed I've born the brunt.

Death & The Neofeudal Media Platform Overlord

DEATH:

Just what did you think?
What brink did you sink?
D'you really think that all can be linked
before I came your brain to tame?

OVERLORD:

We started well the world connection
but ended selling information.
I never cared about complexion
until the likes my dope did spike.
Oh, how I long of it to be rid!
(I don't even give it to my kid.)

Death & The Poet

DEATH...

It's done. You've lost.
Your fleet of words are fleeting.

Don't talk. Spell not
(unless to me a greeting).

Your boast is most peculiar in an age where rage becomes you.

Where language lingers, a lame game, its lineaments still hum blue.

POET:

...

Death & The Data Scientist

DEATH...

The data age is not the day to age.
Your mind to me's a tasty wage.
The one last thing you thought to call,
to predict, alas was your downfall.

DATA SCIENTIST:

For others the rotting scroll,
the flow state of the tense neck muscle,
is but a random scrot flate,
forgotten within the daily hustle.
For me this scroll is cuneiform,
a hieroglyphic desire-trace,
a warm numerical yearn
patterned like the sand of ancient races.

& Death to Death

DEATH...

Good one, good one, I'm always here
from very beginning to end of days.
For how can I to I appear?
Can the sun see its own rays?

DEATH:

Behind beginnings and after ends,
there's no rough chance you'll always be-
coming again but between rends
time, you're gone, in only glee.

The clue in the skies
Flew beyond eyes
Wistful in all sending
Grow on and wenden:
For much lies to create
So don't curl up and wait
For life is your tower
And shivers with power.

THE POET

Child of a German priest and Estonian witch, Mark studied Theology in Oxford and is now based in Exeter where he is doing a PhD in Comparative Culture. He has worked in humanitarian aid and chaplaincy. Other selections of his poetry can be found in the Psychedelic Press Journal.

He can be reached on markschunemann@gmail.com

or, on his blog at psychedelictheology.wordpress.com

THE ARTIST

Gabriella grew up in Dorset and from a young age was inspired to write and illustrate books. Reading English Literature at Oxford, she specialised in the medieval period, which continues to be the inspiration for her writing and painting. She continues to live in Oxford, making beautifully-crafted storybooks for all to treasure.

She can be reached at gabriella.bailey@hotmail.co.uk

Milton Keynes UK
Ingram Content Group UK Ltd.
UKHW022201101024
449474UK00008B/80